THE PROMISES OF GLASS

ALSO BY MICHAEL PALMER

BOOKS AND CHAPBOOKS

The Danish Notebook
The Lion Bridge: Selected Poems 1972–1995
At Passages
An Alphabet Underground
For a Reading
Sun
Songs for Sarah
First Figure
Notes for Echo Lake
Alogon
Transparency of the Mirror
Without Music
The Circular Gates
C's Songs
Blake's Newton
Plan of the City of O

SELECTED TRANSLATIONS

Voyelles by Arthur Rimbaud
Jonah Who Will Be 25 in the Year 2000 (film by Alain Tanner)
The Surrealists Look at Art (with Norma Cole)
Blue Vitriol by Alexei Parshchikov (with John High and Michael Molnar)
Theory of Tables by Emmanuel Hocquard
Three Moral Tales by Emmanuel Hocquard
in *The Selected Poetry of Vicente Huidobro*
in *The Random House Book of Twentieth Century French Poetry*
in *Nothing the Sun Could Not Explain: 20 Contemporary Brazilian Poets*
in *Twenty-two New French Writers*

OTHER

Code of Signals: Recent Writings in Poetics, ed. Michael Palmer

MICHAEL PALMER

THE PROMISES OF GLASS

A NEW DIRECTIONS BOOK

Manufactured in the United States of America
New Directions Books are printed on acid-free paper
First published clothbound in 2000
Published simultaneously in Canada by Penguin Books Canada Limited

AUTHOR'S NOTE: I am grateful to the editors of the various magazines in which most of these poems first appeared: *American Letters & Commentary, American Poetry Review, Boston Book Review, Boxkite, Capilano Review, CCCP Review, Chicago Review, Colorado Review, Common Knowledge, Conjunctions, Cut Bank, Faucheuse, Iowa Review, New American Writing, Phoebe, Pressed Wafer, Sagetrieb, Sakura, Sulfur,* and *Zyzzyva.*

Acknowledgment is made as well to the following anthologies: *American Poets Say Goodbye to the Twentieth Century* (ed. Andrei Codrescu, Four Walls, Eight Windows); *Exact Change Annual #1* (ed. Peter Gizzi, Exact Change Press); *The Gertrude Stein Awards in Innovative American Poetry (1995)* (ed. Douglas Messerli, Sun & Moon Press); *The Harvill Book of Twentieth-Century Poetry in English* (ed. Michael Schmidt, The Harvill Press); *Onward: Contemporary Poetry and Poetics* (ed. Peter Baker, Peter Long Publishing); *The Oxford Anthology of American Poetry* (ed. Cary Nelson, Oxford University Press).

"Autobiography" and "Autobiography 2" were first published in *At Passages* (1995) and reprinted in *The Lion Bridge: Selected Poems 1972–1995* (1998). They reappear here as part of the completed sequence.

The poem "In an X" was originally composed for inclusion in the volume *je te continue ma lecture (Mélanges pour Claude Royet-Journaud),* edited by Michèle Cohen-Halimi and Francis Cohen and published in Paris by P.O.L. in 1999.

Library of Congress Cataloging in Publication Data
Palmer, Michael, 1943–
The promises of glass / Michael Palmer.
p. cm.
ISBN 0-8112-1443-5 (alk. paper)
I. Title.
PS3566.A54 P7 2000
813'.54–dc21 99-088019

New Directions Books are published for James Laughlin
by New Directions Publishing Corporation
80 Eighth Avenue, New York 10011

Contents

THE PROMISES OF GLASS

THE WHITE NOTEBOOK

The White Notebook

But we have painted over the chalky folds,
the snow- and smoke-folds, so carefully,
so deftly that many (Did you bet

on the margins, the clouds?) that many
will have gone, unnoticed,
under. Water under water,

"earth that moves beneath earth."
We have added
silver to the river, dots of silver,

red, figures-which-are-not. Tell
me what their names might have been,
what were last and first, what spells

the unfamiliar, awkwardly whispered, syllable?
And what of the blue rider, the Arab
horseman, the *cavalier* composed

of two shades of blue, one
from Vermeer's Delft, the other
from that metallic element called

cobalt, *Kobolt,* goblin? What scene
is he watching? Is it expired space
the fixed eye observes? Is it

the river which has no center, the
whiteness of the city when you say
Paris is white? Is it the arches

of the bridges now narrowed to slits?
Is it the liquid
voices themselves

he watches grow silent?
The voice of closed eyes?
Or the two

impossibly young
in the lighted room
who speak only of rain?

Scene which has no center
or whose center is empty,
elsewhere. The way white is said

rejoining an earlier whiteness
between the done and the not-yet
rolling off the tongue

almond, almond-eyed,
eyeless, denialwhite
as the zero code, wordless,

a language of rhythm and breath.
(In erasure the chestnut
flowering toward origin

among the names for white:
blanc de titane, blanc de zinc.)
I met her there at the crossroads.

I don't remember who spoke.
Two breaths, two patterns of echo.
We have painted a bridge's eyes

narrowed, its mouth spurting sand,
dots, more dots, bright,
not visible to the eye.

River of dots rising,
stream of sand with no center.
This was both before and after.

Palette knife beside a photograph.
At recess the children's cries
through the studio windows,

station clocktower to the right,
ochre of expanding sound,
tongue to mute tongue, tendrils—

tendons—over rooftops.
Didn't it turn me—
he asks of his eye—

didn't it polish me
like one of its stones,
remingle and remake me

and draw me quickly down
to where each night in sand
the hour sounds?

We met there at the crossroads
near the small arcades.

I can't recall who first spoke,
who said, "the darkness of white."

We shared one shadow.
In the heat she tasted of salt.

THE PROMISES OF GLASS

Autobiography

All clocks are clouds.

Parts are greater than the whole.

A philosopher is starving in a rooming house, while it rains outside.

He regards the self as just another sign.

Winter roses are invisible.

Late ice sometimes sings.

A and *Not-A* are the same.

My dog does not know me.

Violins, like dreams, are suspect.

I come from Kolophon, or perhaps some small island.

The strait has frozen, and people are walking—a few skating—across it.

On the crescent beach, a drowned deer.

A woman with one hand, her thighs around your neck.

The world is all that is displaced.

Apples in a stall at the streetcorner by the Bahnhof, pale yellow to blackish red.

Memory does not speak.

Shortness of breath, accompanied by tinnitus.

The poet's stutter and the philosopher's.

The self is assigned to others.

A room from which, at all times, the moon remains visible.

Leningrad cafe: a man missing the left side of his face.

Disappearance of the sun from the sky above Odessa.

True description of that sun.

A philosopher lies in a doorway, discussing the theory of colors

with himself

the theory of self with himself, the concept of number, eternal return, the sidereal pulse

logic of types, Buridan sentences, the *lekton.*

Why now that smoke off the lake?

Word and thing are the same.

Many times white ravens have I seen.

That all planes are infinite, by extension.

She asks, Is there a map of these gates?

She asks, Is this the one called Passages, or is it that one to the west?

Thus released, the dark angels converse with the angels of light.

They are not angels.

Something else.

for Poul Borum

Autobiography 2 (hellogoodby)

The Book of Company which
I put down and can't pick up

The Trans-Siberian disappearing,
the Blue Train and the Shadow Train

Her body with ridges like my skull
Two children are running through the Lion Cemetery

Five travelers are crossing the Lion Bridge
A philosopher in a doorway insists

that there are no images
He whispers instead: Possible Worlds

The Mind-Body Problem
The Tale of the Color Harpsichord

Skeleton of the World's Oldest Horse
The ring of O dwindles

sizzling around the hole until gone
False spring is laughing at the snow

and just beyond each window
immense pines weighted with snow

A philosopher spreadeagled in the snow
holds out his Third Meditation

like a necrotic star. He whispers:
archery is everywhere in decline,

photography the first perversion of our time
Reach to the milky bottom of this pond

to know the feel of bone,
a knuckle from your grandfather's thumb,

the maternal clavicle, the familiar
arch of a brother's brow

He was your twin, no doubt,
forger of the unicursal maze

My dearest Tania, When I get a good position in the courtyard
I study their faces through the haze

Dear Tania, Don't be annoyed,
please, at these digressions

They are soldering the generals
back onto their pedestals

for A. C.

Autobiography 3

Yes, I was born on the street known as Glass—as Paper, Scissors or Rock.

Several of my ancestors had no hands.

Several of my ancestors used their pens

in odd ways.

A child of seven I prayed for breath.

Each day I passed through the mirrored X

into droplets of rain congealed around dust.

I never regretted this situation.

Though patient as an alchemist I failed to learn English.

Twenty years later I burned all my furniture.

Likewise the beams of my house

to fuel the furnace.

Once I bought an old boat.

I abandoned the tyrannical book of my dreams

and wrote about dresses, jewels, furniture and menus

eight or ten times in a book of dreams.

It sets me to dreaming when I dust it off.

Our time is a between time; best to stay out of it.

Send an occasional visiting card to eternity or a few stanzas to the living

so they won't suspect we know they don't exist.

Sign them Sincerely Yours, Warmest Regards, Thinking of You or Deepest Regrets.

Brown river outside my window, an old boat riding the current.

What I like most is to stay in my apartment.

So that is my life, pared of anecdotes.

I go out occasionally to look at a dance.

Otherwise the usual joys, worries and inner mourning.

Occasionally in an old boat I navigate the river

when I find the time.

Water swallows the days.

I think maybe that's all

I have to say

except that an irregular heart sometimes speaks to me.

It says, A candle is consuming a children's alphabet.

It says, Attend to each detail of the future-past.

Last night the moon was divided precisely in half.

Today a terrifying wind.

Autobiography 4 (Idem)

Voice: Do you see that purple tint the sky has taken on?

Other Voice: I'd say mauve, it's more a mauve.

V.: Is there any difference?

O.V.: One has more pink.

V.: Which?

O.V.: Which what?

V.: Which has more pink?

O.V.: I don't really know.

V.: Then how can you . . .

O.V.: It sounds right for that.

V.: Do you always go by the sound?

O.V.: Sound?

V.: The sound, the . . .

O.V.: What does that mean, "Go by the sound"?

V.: I mean sometimes it begins with sounds—nothing else. You follow, you . . .

O.V.: Musical sounds?

V.: No, less organized.

O.V.: Like the sounds around us now?

V.: No, like the sounds not around us now.

O.V.: Sounds you can't hear?

V.: Sounds you can't hear.

O.V.: You listen to sounds you can't hear?

V.: No.

O.V.: No?

V.: It's before listening.

O.V.: Before listening?

V.: Listening is attention. Before attention.

O.V.: *Mauve:* "A delicate purple, violet or lilac color."

V.: *Purple:* "A color of a hue between blue and red; one of the colors commonly called violet, lilac, mauve, etc."

O.V.: Same and not.

V.: Same or not.

O.V.: Same as not.

V.: Not same.

O.V.: Same not same.

V.: The form is fulfilled at thirty-six.

O.V.: Magenta.

Autobiography 5

Not exactly a mark, not exactly a trace.

More like a segment of recording tape.

After I arrived I took a job painting broccoli, cabbage and squash

on supermarket windows

as I was putting on my face:

base, blusher, mascara, ultra high-gloss lip enamel

when the word "*zurückgehen*" flooded my brain

as if spoken by the mirror

over the dressing table in which an image

no longer gathered much light, its

reflecting glaze having decayed.

We were so close that the way

we came apart was not even visible to the participants.

Then I became a painter of paintings briefly

then I eliminated paint.

Dear Phil, What a hellish season it's been.

For a time I thought I was another

but now I'm selling shovels and rakes, running a few guns

and awaiting the arrival

of a photographic apparatus.

Perhaps if a gate deforms in parallax

a phrase will pass through it.

Perhaps if a face can be recorded—

but isn't that another story?

Isn't there another story

consistent with sand?

How it turns to mirror-glass

when heated in your hand.

The sounds it makes

make another story.

It's completely silent here

so we hear nothing but high and low tones

constantly

as we take inventory.

The people come in shades of blue.

They take everything from you.

Autobiography 6

(1)

My name is Johnny Jump-Up
And I live in a shiny car
And when I'm really happy
It takes me very far

Often this most post-modern of songs
runs through my head
Perhaps I should explain
after my fashion

When I play games of cards
I like to shuffle the deck seven times
knowing that at the eighth
as regards randomness

little more is to be gained
I live with Dolores, a sailmaker
who has proven a satisfactory companion
though prone like myself to melancholy

when the winds are not just right
Once I found a book on a table
which changed my entire life
So I moved from the hotel where I was born

to another hotel, less well kept
where lizards lolled in the sun
of a deliquescent solarium
We feared tropical storms

yet set sail frequently nonetheless
perhaps as a kind of test
Dolores explained to me how it is
ships float

Any object that floats
is buoyed upward to some extent
This force is caused by the weight
of the water it displaces—

the water pressure rises with increasing depth
and because the object is subject
to more pressure from below
than from above, it too may rise

(2)

O they call me Johnny Jump-Up
For that is not my name
My head rolled down the marble stairs
Things never stay the same

Our acquaintance M. Collins
would often sing this refrain
from a seat in his favorite cafe
on Escarpment Place

M. Collins it appears came from Chicago
though his accent was no less than perfect
He taught philosophy to idlers
including yours truly

whenever we took shelter from the rain
under the awning of his cafe
It should be noted that M. Collins
has published no books of philosophy

and in fact describes himself
as "a mere table of contents . . .
a very snarl of twine"
Yet on induction and probabilities

he has much to say,
as on indices and icons,
ordinary propositions and the indefinite future
He sang in a lilting tenor

which, given a calm day,
could be heard as far away
as the Library of the Ursulines
in one direction, #10

Street of Modalities in another,
an address which recently appeared to me
in a dream very brief but very clear
The taxi taking you away was a drunken blue

O they called him Johnny Jump-Up
Since that was not his name
His head rolled down the marble stairs
All this is really true

Autobiography 7

You go out for a walk in the rain.
You make love in the rain.

These are not the same
acts. It might or might not

be the same rain. The in
might be two different ins,

one an under, one a during.
You sell fish of gold for a living,

not goldfish, not living fish.
You make a poor living.

It rains day and night
causing the river to rise

and flood your knick-knack shop.
You can step into this river twice

unlike the river of life.
Unlike the river of life

this is a real river, brown and turbid,
with many objects in it.

Today I count: a drowned dog,
short-haired and of medium size;

an office chair, the kind that squeaks
when you lean back; the head of a stag

mounted on oak; endless mattresses
stained and striped like cheap ties;

a tongue-and-groove door lacking its knob;
a superannuated perambulator

such as I was paraded in as a child
by my mother in her cardigan, her blue

cotton skirt and sensible shoes;
the fractured limb of a buckeye

tree, whose fruit will paralyze
the nerves and lead to death;

an oar, a doll, an ice chest,
a camper shell and pesticide cans.

But what of these shadow-flowers with yellow stems?
What of panthers in the skins of men?

Autobiography 8

You must have me confused with myself
Yet the clouds open

and flood the language of the dream
the space around the bed

the minute depression
where many before you have slept

Outside, up and somewhat to the left
is the cafe known as The Method

altered now to A Descriptive Method
which starts with a poem and ends with a story

though not the story of the poem
nor the story of the Invisible Translator

with his famous, piercing, azure gaze
his slender fingers raising the cup

of Ceylonese tea (*saveur de menthe*)
empaqueté au Sri Lanka

et importé au Canada par
C.C.W. Candy Dist. Inc.

Dorion, Québec J7V 5V8
and thence to the U.S.A.

by Emerson Marketing Co. Inc.
Emerson, New Jersey 07630

circuitous voyage to the teapot
of simple white porcelain

not the philosopher's teapot
(as in fact we call it)

but a gift of the philosopher
who first gently inquired

Do you not own a teapot?
to which I replied

Dottore, on the ashes of Gramsci
in the name of Averroes

on the limbs of Osiris
and the grave of Herakleitos

on the razor of Ockham
I swear I do not

Autobiography 9

(1)

The last two moments went by very fast.
In 1943 I composed my Bagatelles

for harmonica of glass.
Max Jacob once introduced me to an extraordinary woman

who told my fortune.
There are certain things you can't just make up.

Everything had changed by July.
Those of us who were to survive

buried our songs in rows
where I imagine they still lie

or else enclosed them in walls.
I've never attempted to recover those songs.

I've never attempted to remember those songs,
shameful, half-witted songs

enamored of shot light,
empty codex in a darkened house

caught among its sounds
as the fortuneteller said.

(2)

You ask
Did we dance and dance beneath the death's-head clock

and I will not say we did not
You ask

Did you visit the Hypnotist to the Stars
but I cannot say we noticed any stars

She asked
Have you lived for long in this odd house of air

but I could not tell whether she meant
this stone, or that one over there

beneath which we buried
the future of the past

its shawls and cups and tones
Since you ask

here is a syllable spoken only once
and here a garden of smoke

Here is a well with no bottom at all
and in this well we dance

Autobiography 10

"Autobiography 10" has disappeared. In fact, I have no memory of whether it ever existed. I noticed its absence while returning to "Autobiography 9" today (23 September 1997) to complete some long-intended revisions. Perhaps in its place I should refer readers to my essay of many years ago, "Autobiography, Memory and Mechanisms of Concealment."

The Metaphysician of Prague

(Autobiography 11)

The Metaphysician of Prague whom
I will call Quod, short for Quodlibet.

Do you remember do you recall
Quod, his corpse at the lock? Quod as dust?

Quod the Transparent? Quod the empty
elegist? Quod in love? Quod in love

with the sentence? Quod in love with an
enormous breast, suspended, illu-

minated, overhead? Quod the Per-
plexed? Quod, his dream by the burning well?

Quod at the work of possible worlds
and among the young girls? Quod and the

watch, stopped (Quod of Departures)? Hundred
Headless Quod in search of time past in

a forest of glass? Quod the Obscure?
Quod the Stammerer? Inebriate,

incurious Quod of the vacant
hours? Quod of the marsh, the samphire, the

scallop and crab, cloud, the hut of reeds?
Quod of night, Quod of fog, Quod of the

single eye, the braided tongue? Quod the
Metaphrast, the Leveller, the Frac-

tionist? Quod in a mist, at the bridge?
Anaclitic Quod? Seated, with jug?

Quod the Erect? Quod, his abjection?
Quod of the customshouse? Quod the Mute?

Saint Quod of the Forgotten Paradox?
Quod of the fragment, at the crossroads

where the lovers meet? His lies and withered
lungs? Quod at the street of screams? Quod, his

vertigo, his works and days, numbers
and names? Quod of the paper house, the

wind through that house? Quod before a door?
Quod of the last light, the soil that shifts?

And Quod whiter than white, whiter than
the page? Do you remember the page?

The Subject

(Autobiography 12)

It is not true that I (the subject) is
    formally opposed to pleasure—even to extremes
    of pleasure—as has been recently adduced.

Still, in a landscape of murderous rapture—
    skin peeling back from their faces—
    where clouds may seem to resemble

caricatures of the *philosophes* playing bumpercars
    it is well to remember
    how in moments of early childhood blindness

we will be roused
    by a visit, entirely unforeseen,
    from Our Lady of the Balloons

and how reacting to this
    we (the subject, collectively) will wheeze
    in classic paroxysm. Your

mouth begins to feel funny,
    then hands and wrists commence to itch,
    then your crotch and armpits.

Your eyes and lips swell
    and hives puff out
    across your entire body.

Lungs quickly fill,
    blood-pressure falls
    and heartbeat wildly accelerates.

You are nearing death now
    allergic to
    the violent alternations

of hue,
    orbital red,
    silver, blue

rending the visual field,
    once the white of a final
    whiteness where

from your window you could see
    a stone suspended in air
    and on it an ancient city.

Autobiography 13

The hand has numbers on it.
A plane, a propeller plane, is

crossing the sky. If you connect the dots
a hand is crossing the sky

a hand with numbers on it
is waving hello and goodby.

How vexing to the interpreters
who have forgotten how to sleep.

Here, try these, my new glasses.
Note that I have painted the lenses black

as ink. In my pocket I carry a crystal heart
which throbs to an erratic beat.

Remember, at the hour of the rose
the rose will rewrite itself

in liquid redder than ink,
claimed the mayor of our fading town

before plunging from Lovers' Leap.
Such were the passions of democracy.

He landed on a page of paper
near picnickers in a verdant field.

This page of paper is my child,
alas now dead, the mayor exclaimed

brushing blood and bone from foot and head,
and it is for me to become an architect.

I will build you a city on a hill.
Peppertrees will line its streets

and its citizens all will be Jane and Bill,
daughters and sons of palmistry.

On the rude wings of storm
machines that fly will be borne

aloft, carrying you, Jane, and you, Bill,
and music will play of its own will.

São Paulo Sighs

(Autobiography 14)

Lembras-te?
Mário de Andrade

Our sighs in São Paulo
sounded something like this:

a kiss is just a kiss
be it rain or simply mist

The animal alphabet
passed overhead

with its twenty-three wings
rhythm-a-ning a samba for the dead

We walked and walked and we saw:
a rock star without his rock,

two pictures of a rose in the dark
We saw: the shorn locks of a nun

beside an abandoned well
and we peered into our porous hearts

where militiamen secretly dwell
We walked and walked, we three

the Professor of Everything,
the Professor of Nothing

and yours very truly
We witnessed:

the theoretical arrival
of the workers' paradise

by means of its statuary
We examined a woman's skeleton perfectly drawn

skeleton of everything,
skeleton of nothing

on a blue-lit barroom wall
and we noted the sun's

utter failure to explain
anything at all

regarding the mist and the rain
There's no cosmic close-out on raincoats

no discount on drizzles
so you must remember this

When São Paulo sighs
a kiss is just a kiss

for Régis Bonvicino

And Sighs Again

(Autobiography 15)

A sea of small killings, invisibilities, precise
scents of night

in its wetness
its edges of bloom

and inflection
A woman, chestnut-fleshed, nipples erect, ascends a kind of cross

Her companion, her double, her accomplice in this
helps her rise up with her tongue

Out of the dark they are fashioning a rose,
a window

They are examining the mathematics of the fold
They are baking themselves in salt

that we of little faith
may be saved

from the dampness and the dark
They are writing a book of common knowledge

a book of maxims and proverbs
such as a father

might pass on to a son
Did I say father and son

when I meant
farther and farther from the sun

Did I say fold
when I meant fault

salt when I meant song
dark when I meant a little bark

steering straight into the storm
Boat, little boat

with sail of stone,
Are you bearing an alphabet

among the rats in your hold,
an A-B-C-D of twinned bodies

Is the skin of this city your own,
city over which another city floats

skin of a retinal machine
salt sea of invisibilities

Second Night Song

(Autobiography 16)

Snail we saw
edging along a sentence

There was rain and its grammar
of outline and shadow

Arkadii are you counting
the shards of shattered glass

The Promises of Glass

(Autobiography 17)

Will be will have been
That singing in the streets or was it screams

and the tangos of exile
tangos of asylum

beneath the blue-flowering trees—
pawlonias I believe—fractured

lines veiling eyes—
maple, then poplar, then ash—

as she recites
Will be will have been

as she recites
The new book the new life

book of the half-light
of storm as you arrive

There will be will have been
the book made of books

and how it speaks—
reeds, moist earth, myosotis—

the promises of leaves
and the promises of glass

(book of the burning wells
book of the spinning lens)

Near dawn the letters dance
through the door again

under earth's rim
It's a dance that spreads like a fan

dance some would say of the jubilant crowd
the transparent stones, the particle rose

dance some would say of the hanging man
tattered shirt, worn boots, silly grin

Will be will have been
We greet the severed music

in the meantime
and the name of

This new pen hardly works at all
Grace notes and ghost notes bouncing off the walls

Picture

(Autobiography 18)

If "on a stair"
and gazing through glass
                                        if there...

A picture held us captive
How did I think that

What did I think
A cry, a laugh

a doodle on a page
and the stewpot too

can see and hear
can truly see and hear
                                    if there

If shadow, a form
if thought, a ladder

if pain, whose pain
You think that after all

a candle will be enough
but it won't be enough

(it wasn't enough)
a word will be enough

but which word will be enough
A ghost, a Pierrot, a street

are not enough
A mirror on a stage

has never been enough
a shard, a fable, a shroud

a rose—a red rose—in the dark,
strict spiral on a lake of salt

It's true I wasted the day
watching the waterfowl

arrive and depart
the Canada geese, black swans

cormorants and eider ducks,
lilies and rose mallows in the marsh

True as well as not true
True as well as not

Now say the word "fault"
Then stare at this mark

for Ann Lauterbach

Q

Quod reflects
upon the amulet

of ancient glass
from Castra

the necklace
of eye beads

the cosmetic flask
colored pendants

of melting faces
from Maresha

***

Quod reflects:

There among the columns
they're speaking a lost language
of sibilants and clicks

a forgotten language
there above the sparks
of passing streetcars

***

Quod in Nighttown

stumbling up the stairs
or was it down

***

She holds him thus
then guides him in

***

Quod before Minos

(Quod among the cries
from the second circle)

***

Dixit Quod:

This elegant casket
stitched at the spine

***

Quod in the New World

with his new toothbrush
designated *extra soft*

***

Announces to the gathering

in San Francisco that he has
discovered the perfect number

***

Quod considers:

the idea of a Dino Burger
at the La Brea Diner

***

Quod at the gate
fumbling for his key

It's late
It's the wrong key

***

Quod's dream
of the darkest of colors

Bodies lean
into the lost meanings

of head and tongue and arm
their movements

forgetful of time
Yet the painter—

that figure unremarked
until now—

will decide at the last
to paint these bodies out

***

Q glances

                sideways
at the dancers

***

Q devours

the biographies
of owls

***

Very late
Quod waits

to hear
his voice speak

***

Quod wonders whether it might ever be possible to slip completely free of thought; thought that has raveled him since his earliest years, whether awake or asleep; thought that has become, lacking any option, his profession.

***

At the next moment (accepting for a moment the fiction of a *next* moment), Quod considers the possibility that he is no longer a thinker, if indeed he ever was one, but has become instead merely a performer of thought or, even worse, a professor of thought.

***

To Elsa

from Prague
Quod writes:

Quit Paris
and come

Or are you no longer
"living in freedom"

***

Quod's final sighting
of Mayakovsky
by the Charles Bridge

(Quod who
in a letter
to Elsa

now admits
he himself
"does not exist")

***

But at what age—
he can't remember—

did the light-cloud arrive
to blind him

***

Quod wonders:
Am I the first

metaphysician
to fall down this

spiral of steps
while counting them

***

The mirror that delivers Quod backward in time, and the mirror that reflects the present upon him, are one and the same. Then there is the mirror of the future which, because of its extreme age, has lost its tain and thus become incapable of harboring images.

***

Quod sleeps beneath the scarlet lips of Man Ray's The Hour of the Observatory in a borrowed apartment half a kilometer or so from the observatory itself and down the street from what was once Man Ray's studio. These near congruences remind him how once, in an adjacent quarter of the same city, he observed a young woman as she applied a like color to her lips before departing for the final time, except from his sleep to which she would return periodically for many years, regardless of the hour of the night.

***

And there once again
a few hundred steps

from Beckett's grave
Quod craves

a second starless
inscrutable hour

***

And the graves of Tzara, Ionesco, Jean Seberg, Soutine, Zadkine, Henri Langlois, Sarah Kofman, Sartre and de Beauvoir, Dreyfus, César Franck, Fargue, Saint-Beuve, Laurens, Baudelaire sharing a stone with his mother and the Général Aupick. He cannot, however, locate Vallejo. That evening, at dinner with four friends, one asks, "But what about Vallejo—none of us can seem to find him?"

***

The bombs, Quod notes

fall where they may
whatever the leaders say

***

Traveling north from Heathrow by bus in the early morning mist, Quod notices a straw-colored pig in a muddy field, a raven perched astride its back.

Later the same day, at the Fitzwilliam, a still-life of five apples.

And that night, in a slippage of time, Quod watches through the branches in the park as his mother is led to a waiting van.

***

Idly scanning the channels
Quod reflects on the time

when his writings were banned
and his readers many

***

At a movie theater to watch—whatever. More important, the invisibility and darkness. Night "numbered, avid and secretly organized." The rustle of others.

***

On his birthday Quod notes that his age this year constitutes a prime number:

He envisions
the Sieve
of Eratosthenes

***

Buries Quince the Cat beneath the hawthorn. Strayhorn on the penny-whistle. So long.

***

Bees swarm. Quod

lost among them
attempts to hum.

FOUR KITAJ STUDIES

Prose for the World's Body

Perhaps there is danger; perhaps
it was only a creak
in the floorboards. Perhaps a
body will have entered, is
about to depart, the frame.
A socket lacking a bulb.
Hanger hanging by its shadow.
Redness of this interior, not
blood-red, not bloodless, not a
remembered red. But an inflection.
He means to say that
there are so many books
we have lost count of
the books that are not.
On the cover of this
one, who will say, though
he cannot. He absolutely cannot—
will not. On the cover
of this one, a table
with daubs and tubes, brushes,
bottles, canisters and cans. On
the cover of this one,
a melancholy aphorist, a whore
with green hair and red
leggings, a sweeper. A man
lies dead in the street.
Maybe it is Schulz. Perhaps
they are unaware of this.
Perhaps he was shot while
they were coming. Behind the
sweeper, to our left, a
woman in a yellow dress
is hailing a cab. Here
Benjamin says, It's blood itself,
it's a stain on a

wall, even a lexicon. One,
the man called The Singer,
will be in hiding, will
live beneath the streets. Perhaps
they are unaware of this.
Perhaps they cannot hear any
sounds from the streets. Do
not wish to hear. As
we ourselves routinely disregard them.
He means to say to
her, It is nothing, only
a creak in the floorboards,
moth at the windowpane, a
pulse. It is no one.

If Not, Not

They tell each other stories,
lies composed as dreams and
always in the colors of
dreams: rust, chrome yellow, coral,
chemical green. Of the dying
figures, loosely assembled, by a
riverbank. The gatehouse. A journey
by train through beautiful countryside,
indescribable countryside. I was there
cut in half, only to
survive. A young dancer, standing
at the third-floor window. Cobalt
blue, argentine, bone white. What
we called that hour in
those days. He means to
say that on that same
hill Goethe and Eckermann would
sometimes walk. "Always the old
story, always the old bed
of the sea!" He means
to say, The music of
moths, the small lamps. She
stares from the window on
the third floor, toward the
square below. He says, These
are yellow-hammers and sparrows, but
there are no larks. Come
Whitsuntide, the mockingbird and the
yellow thrush will arrive. Here
at the heart, a small
pond, stagnant in the shadow
of smoke. The late flowers.

The Questions of Crows

There is dust. Are we
to love the dust? There
are shadows. Will we make
a tent of shadows, a
shelter of black rivulets? The
scholar bends over his text
a final time. He is
counting the library's limbs, the
cobwebs, the number of sounds
till the end. He is
looking for something infinitely small,
something that has no size,
but his eyes are bad.
When he uses his eyes
he finds a dot—too
large; an invisible vowel—too
loud. Eyes closed he sees:
heartthread, seahair, stigma, ferry and
ferryman, and the almond-eyed, beneath.
Sees: the dancers circling in
rings, marchers in their rows.
Hears the questions of crows:
Are we to love the
dust? Make tents of shadows?

Study

In a darkened room they
speak as one against the
religion of the word, against
the prophetic, the sublime, the
orphic call. It is a
strange conversation, coming as it
does after hours of making
love, mid-afternoon till now, at
this their second meeting, shutters
closed to block the lamplight
outside. Seated on the bed,
the curve of her back
toward him, she is smoking.
It is unclear whether they
believe what they are saying.

FIVE EASY POEMS

for Anne-Marie Albiach

Note

In the summer of 1982, I went to the Hôtel de l'Odéon in Paris in the hope of meeting the poet Anne-Marie Albiach. She was for the moment in residence there, but without a phone, and Claude Royet-Journoud had suggested I simply drop by and try my luck. I had first read her book *État* in the nineteen-seventies, and it had seemed a perfect work, a work perfectly realized and perfectly necessary. It had filled a space in the poetic imagination of the time that had until then been awaiting it, unoccupied.

At the Hôtel de l'Odéon, the poet Anne-Marie Albiach was not in, so I left a copy of my *Notes for Echo Lake* for her with the desk clerk and departed. After my initial disappointment, I gradually began to comprehend that this had been a most excellent first meeting with the poet Anne-Marie Albiach. Neither had failed to meet the expectations of the other. The poet Anne-Marie Albiach had been spared the *embuscade* of *gaucheries* and malaproprian ejaculations with which it is my habit to greet the French. Our conversation, in short, had never deviated from the highest plane. And, as is the case with absence generally, a trace of the erotic had lingered in the atmosphere, at least from my point of view.

This non-encounter (or what the post-structuralist might term this "in-place-of-an-encounter") served further to spur a series of reflections on the *odéon,* that is the odeum, that public space for theater and the performance of poetry from which, these days, poets not infrequently find themselves excluded. Such reflections have continued to the present.

Now these "Five Easy Poems," dedicated with love to Anne-Marie Albiach on her sixtieth birthday.

Two pictures of a rose in the dark
A woman wounded on the street

has been carried in
a woman with wounds to the upper arm and neck

has been brought to the room where our clocks
seem always to stop

The room itself is dark
This question of the clocks

she might say, of points on the clock
and in the dark

pauses and addictions, colors
of the moment

voices, glances and nervous hands
The river below the window—

river as it's pictured
on a field without perspective—

is red
a film of smoke and mist

hanging over it
As if asleep while writing this

Two pictures of a rose in the dark
We say one is lost one is not

or one is a syllable one a stone
They ask and they ask

Picture of who picture of what
It has been reported

in the ploughed field
amid today's crop:

buttons, shards of a bowl
flange of an eye-socket

flexed torso of a child
the pages of a diary

folded in her cloak
We do not say of the sky

that it is an arena for dance
that it is a blue stream gently flowing

or that at the end of the dream
a flower will remain

of an identical blue
We do not say we partly sing

back toward the whir
and the whistling of things

It is as it was in the film
He guides the beads into and out of her

while eddies of dust
rise from the hooves of a riderless horse

turning in a circle
She fingers the beads into then out of him

counting from one to a thousand and one
They attain:

a perfect knowledge of the fragment
and the discourse of liquid surfaces

They attain:
anamnesis as regards the scent of apples,

apricots and pears
They understand:

the Paradox of the Knower
and the Paradox of the Stone,

Paradox of the Hangman, Paradox of the Heap,
and the one of the Circling Horse

It is as it was in the film
The worriers worry the beads

The camera shuttles nervously
Eddies of dust rise up

(mezza voce)

Does he incline his head to become calligraphy,
memory of his body's desire

for the moving letters of an alphabet
of intractable geometry, Ariadne's thread

as the trickling of warm blood?
Is the head bent in reminiscence,

thought of distance, arteries'
incandescence, first witness,

precision of a gesture?
Of which a trace remains

at a certain distance.
At a certain distance

twin bodies encircle a letter
they have arrived at independently

during the one night
of a thousand and one.

What language is the Chorus speaking
from which words do not come?

What is the space
of the odeum?

All poems
are easy poems

It's just that some
are even easier

than others
These we call

the easiest poems
of all

IN AN X

In an X

for (and after) Claude Royet-Journoud

1. I describe this as if it were before me it is not before me.

2. I say it is a picture it is not a picture.

3. I say it is a picture of a thing it is not a picture not a thing it is not a picture of a thing.

4. I say I remember it as if it were yesterday I do not remember it I do not remember yesterday.

5. While in Belo Horizonte the clouds

6. I say I am borne on the back of an elephant formed by the bodies of maidens.

7. There, pages of glass.

8. I say there is a girl with a gold chain around her naked waist.

9. I say that I have seen a rose a red rose in the dark this is not the case.

10. I say that I am in pain.

11. I say this question of the center interests me very much where center is the center of an X.

12. We say space this space where all we have done is raise the question of space.

13. Space or a possible space where the streets are reflected in a mirror and a polished metal disc projects the light of the sky upon the scene at a corner of the deserted square.

14. Sky now citrine and slowly lowering.

15. I describe this as if it were before me.

16. It is not a picture not a sky.

17. While on Nansensgade Claude the sun continues to grow.

18. Though we must ask: this sun or that sun or a complicity of suns.

19. I say this question of dissolution interests me very much.

20. I say I look at the sea the sky I write every day.

21. Upon the word a table upon the table nightbook by nightlight.

22. This house—did I mention the name of this house?

23. Did I not say, My task was to be a sower of eyes!

24. So I'm a dying swan and I'm singing a song.

25. So I'm long gone.

*****

26. The time the blue takes crossing to white.

27. I describe this as if it were inside it is not inside.

28. Crowded onto the colorwheel as it turns.

29. I say not a picture but the thought of a picture it is not a picture not a thought.

30. We say science or silence of the song.

31. We say from the voice the body from the mark the page.

32. Hand waving in the wind there is no arm.

33. I describe this as if it were before me it is before me.

34. I describe this as if it were before me it is before me in the dark.

35. By in the dark I mean: he unjoins his hands/employs them in the cipher.

36. By in the dark I mean: enclose the noise/of another tongue.

37. By in the dark I mean: taken apart and put back together by thought.

38. By in the dark I mean: before the war meaning in the dark.

39. Our onetime world is lost in night.

40. A crime committed by the page or hidden by the page.

41. Our onetime world swallowed by the page.

42. My body as a diagram of the body the body of another.

43. Body of the text goes the phrase.

44. Swallower of alphabets goes the phrase.

45. Dancing in the dark goes the phrase.

46. Paper house goes the phrase from a grammar that's been lost.

47. House with four walls no ceiling or floor.

48. Water pouring in.

49. Books shut.

50. Perpetual surface.

*****

51. I can say the sun is up it is cold out my thoughts are confused.

52. The young platinum-colored cat is howling intermittently.

53. Yesterday I spoke with Dominique about a certain project a secret project will it remain secret.

54. One apple, pale yellow, remaining on the tree, haws of the hawthorn bright orange, harsh low late fall light almost obliterating the page.

55. The feral parrots (Canary-Wings) screeching in the Monterey pine.

56. Two lines from Khlebnikov:

    Russia, I give you my divine
    White brain. Be me. Be Khlebnikov.

57. A fragment from Merleau-Ponty (see 12 above, 13 above).

58. From L.W., *Remarks on Colour,* "We could paint semi-darkness in semi-darkness."

59. America I give you
    my cantaloupe of a brain.
    Do not be me. Be Khlebnikov.

60. L.W., *Remarks on Colour,* "A smooth white surface can reflect things: But what, then, if we made a mistake and that which appeared to be reflected in such a surface were really behind it and seen through it?"

61. "We speak of a 'black mirror'..."

62. Do you love the X or the center more or the idea of a center an invisible center?

63. Exactly midday, pen leaking blue ink onto hand and page.

64. Exhausted from last night's turbulent dreams: A voice saying, Have you never seen the guts of a water buffalo exploding across a rice pond? Have you never watched a tiger as it gnawed on the burnt corpse of a child?

65. At a nearby café for an afternoon coffee, I recognize a familiar neighborhood figure as he descends the street, muttering incomprehensibly or sometimes crying out, and turning every few yards while crossing himself.

66. Walking that is as if not moving at all, or moving forward and in place all at once, sole inhabitant of the circle.

67. Teapot, gift from the Italian philosopher a few years ago, of the simplest white porcelain.

68. No memory without a phantasm.

69. Working that is completely in the present, in the presence of objects, obstacles, this day.

70. So night begins its descent, along the axis of reason.

71. Along the axis of paradox.

72. Along the axis of certainty.

73. Along the axis of doubt.

74. Along the axis of symmetry.

75. A clue, a crime, a body no one can find.

*****

76. While

77. in

78. Belo

79. the

80. rain

81. roar

82. the

83. axial

84. song:

85. Hamnet

86. do

87. not

88. weep

89. Hamnet

90. do

91. not

92. wait

93. Hamnet

94. do

95. not

96. wonder

97. Hamnet

98. do

99. not

100. wake

TOWER

Anode (20 XII 94)

By that fractured lion in the park
was it, our latent memories recombined
so that even the smallest of them—

the one of dust, the one
of a quartzite pebble on a gravestone—
were irretrievably lost.

As sounds in the mouth get lost.
As a traveler—a visitor—may grow silent
in the spaces of a house.

Sun-flares drape the page now
with the purest of lies
in place of desired rains.

Yet it has begun to rain
after all. Is that what you said?
Begun to rain after all?

Anode (27 XII 94)

The words she spoke in sleep
That the city would disappear
In winter a walk through the Summer Gardens

We all recognize ourselves in *Stanzas*
Peter, as in a lake of ice
blue as a lake of ice

or as indigo Eros transfixed by Psyche
Then a tune on a fiddle, inexplicable
you said, how the fingers still play

when frozen like that
fingers of stone like that
beside a lake of ice

A thing is missing we'll never find
Is it made of sleep we ask
Does it carry across the ice

Anode (27 VIII 96 – 26 V 99)

What shadow lights
the buddings of salt

spiral of rock
syntax of rust

grammar of bone
fistfuls of dust

(to the travelers—L.M., N.C.)

Call

If I do not watch the printer it will print a thing I
recognize not.
His sunglasses shattered he threw them into the Lake of
Lost Souls or Last Songs.

I recognized the lake.
In winter it freezes this is not winter.

In that bleak season we don our skates and carve
intricate patterns into the ice, patterns
absolutely precise, and into the air jagged lines.
By the side of the lake we take tea disguised as
Moravian beer.

We watch the bent fisherman in his skiff, couples idling
amid the willows and loosestrife, rehearsing for a
thing not yet known.
My eyes burn from the glare.

Still I recognize the woman seated opposite.
Her eyes are almond-shaped, almost almond-hued, a color
I can't quite name.

She calls me by a name I don't recognize as ever having
been one of mine.
The play is it going well have they learned their parts
shouldn't you be getting back.

Did you rewrite the first act.
Do you know the Canal District the warehouses there.

Man set afire.
Belongings beside him.

Look how that one's tossing her hair.
I had a professor long ago who spoke of perfect
symmetries.

He asked me to his cottage by the sea.
Now you must really leave besides I'm afraid we'll be
seen.

They glide across the mirror surface of the lake, singly
and in pairs, no music except the click of their
skates.
She is practicing her figured eights.

Coil

"Sad coil of streets emitted by a scream."
Dinning of swallows beneath the eaves.

But if you want her, just take her
in exchange for yourself.

Why else The Body Exchange,
Sinaloa at South Paradise,

in the shadow of the glistening thighs
and breasts of the Pussycat Triple X

where all biographies come to an end?
And above us the comet still, though

ever invisible and forever misnamed.
Did I read last week that it was a body

of silently burning ice, strictly indifferent
to the code of names? Or was that some other

object, some other sky, for example the blue
freedom of a shop window

considered absolute because considered true?
So many questions, yet no one

to respond. You in the third row
would you please say something—anything—

also shut up. That's better.
I see now through the stage lights

that you and your companions
are fashioned of etched and tinted glass

of a kind popular in the twenties
that would shatter at the slightest impact

as of high note or hammer.
We pick up the pieces as best we can

and place them with our blood in a box.
Surely all the nights of our lives

have been spent like this
groping along featureless halls

among faces we fail to recognize.
Some have crowded onto the landing

outside, for a smoke, maybe also to scan
once again the night sky.

The one you are looking for, however,
has already departed with another

or dissolved into another,
pick one.

Ballad of Necessities

The moon has been sheared
and so this medicine is good

for nightmares, good for salt tears.
Haven't we watched them grow and glow

in bubbles of cadmium white for years
until a space takes shape at last

not to be measured or known?
Was that or wasn't that the goal?

There's a torso bent double—a woman's—
in a cage of infinite size,

infinitely large and infinitely small,
whose bars are bleached bones.

There's a coven of witches
sullen and bored, hiking their skirts

and hopping across stones,
a feral pig with the head of a dog,

a troll whose ears sprout thorny twigs,
whose curses are songs

of the undoing of form
and of bringing to harm.

All these things we make real for what reason
coloring their eyes an acid green

and forking their swollen tongues?
It's a question never again

to be asked. Just leave them, our shadows, to sing
awful words and dance.

for Augusta

Lens

You are identical with a wooden match
An ace of spades has fallen from the pack

onto a surface both curved and flat
while visitors pass in the heat outside

unaware of the players of cards
faded figures who are photographs

Does speech break on their lips
at the outside corner of either eye

Do they know the edge where the body ends
Did we listen to part song through a lens

Well

How to make love with
a watch on your wrist

There's a stone inside a well,
a folded text

Hawthorn, white oak
woodpecker, mockingbird

The daughter and the son
Who's gone and who's to come

Song inside a wall
"Small house in a large wood"

Winding streets with foreign names
And as for sleep

spelled without letters
it dreams of itself

Stanza

"A ringing in your left ear..."

Some of the books can't be found
and likewise certain rooms

with words in them
or built of words

appear to have been sealed
Sealed against what? First

light perhaps, nails of the hand

tendering the spine a glance
Rain must have its place, its chance

at the music—text
now lost, now gone

Does distance cause the call

Do nights spin

I Do Not

"Je ne sais pas l'anglais."
Georges Hugnet

I do not know English.

I do not know English, and therefore I can have nothing to
say about this latest war, flowering through a night-
scope in the evening sky.

I do not know English and therefore, when hungry, can do no
more than point repeatedly to my mouth.

Yet such a gesture might be taken to mean any number of
things.

I do not know English and therefore cannot seek the requisite
permissions, as outlined in the recent protocol.

Such as: May I utter a term of endearment; may I now proceed
to put my arm or arms around you and apply gentle
pressure; may I now kiss you directly on the lips; now
on the left tendon of the neck; now on the nipple of
each breast? And so on.

Would not in any case be able to decipher her response.

I do not know English. Therefore I have no way of
communicating that I prefer this painting of nothing to
that one of something.

No way to speak of my past or hopes for the future, of my
glasses mysteriously shattered in Rotterdam, the statue
of Eros and Psyche in the Summer Garden, the sudden,
shrill cries in the streets of São Paulo, a watch
abruptly stopping in Paris.

No way to tell the joke about the rabbi and the parrot, the
bartender and the duck, the Pope and the porte-cochère.

You will understand why you have received no letters from me
and why yours have gone unread.

Those, that is, where you write so precisely of the
confluence of the visible universe with the invisible,
and of the lens of dark matter.

No way to differentiate the hall of mirrors from the meadow
of mullein, the beetlebung from the pinkletink, the
kettlehole from the ventifact.

Nor can I utter the words science, seance, silence, language
and languish.

Nor can I tell of the aboreal shadows elongated and shifting
along the wall as the sun's angle approaches maximum
hibernal declination.

Cannot tell of the almond-eyed face that peered from the
well, the ship of stone whose sail was a tongue.

And I cannot report that this rose has twenty-four petals,
one slightly cancred.

Cannot tell how I dismantled it myself at this desk.

Cannot ask the name of this rose.

I cannot repeat the words of the Recording Angel or those of
the Angle of Erasure.

Can speak neither of things abounding nor of things
disappearing.

Still the games continue. A muscular man waves a stick at a ball. A woman in white, arms outstretched, carves a true circle in space. A village turns to dust in the chalk hills.

Because I do not know English I have been variously called Mr. Twisted, The One Undone, The Nonrespondent, The Truly Lost Boy, and Laughed-At-By-Horses.

The war is declared ended, almost before it has begun.

They have named it The Ultimate Combat between Nearness and Distance.

I do not know English.

Tower

Awake way into the night
while the metaphor of clouds sailed by
or should we say slowed by

stole by snowed by
darkest left to darkest right
and zones of time likewise

and a milky stone folded into time.
Time was I was a jelly donut,
the unconsoled, the sadly drooling heart

born with the evil one beside my bed
or maybe not. Time was
I could see the pencil but not the letters

yet thing by thing I began to see again
and my heart grew strong
and became a woman's heart,

a philosopher's heart. Here
are the letters m and a, just now,
the k of cat, the s of table,

just now, wind and racing sky,
the distant cathedral of Epifan',
and after repeating the words pine

then pond a few so many
times I wrote them down
just now and the word crocodile,

and Beograd, Priština, this night their fires.
Time was I would memorize
each thing that passed before my eyes

and scribe it on the magic list,
sleep's deeply secret tablet,
titled *My Life as a Futurist.*

Untitled (May '99)

The dance of the three-legged man
O yes I remember that

his many-colored coat his
hat I remember that

better even than my own
name if not as well

as the required equations
implanted in my youth

that youth I'm now told
I never actually had

and better than the rumble of streetcars
causing our beds to tremble

even as the heavy guns
approach the city's crumbling walls

guns that remind us of harpsichords
plucking out their variations

seemingly once again for a final time
one last dance three-legged man

Quax the Hard Luck Pilot

This light must be coming from somewhere

The Führer was watching Broadway Melody 1940
one of his special favorites

its moments of pure ontology

The cherries are a little late this season
due to prevailing conditions

Still it's better
than no weather at all

The crowds were following an arrow
pointing up toward the sky

So we went along
It seemed only natural

Who knew what we might find

a thousand dancers on unicycles
an aria in a bright vaulted space

eros and thanatos in any case

Or maybe we were there just for the ride

Good Evening Jenny Warmest Greetings Lili and Leni

Some nights I would screen the same
film three or four times

I Ellerkamp his projectionist